The Earth Belongs to All of Us

You Can Make a Difference!

Mary Stanowicz-Freeman

The Earth Belongs to All of Us

You Can Make a Difference!

ARCHWAY
PUBLISHING

Scripture taken from the Holy Bible, NEW INTERNATIONAL
VERSION®. Copyright © 1973, 1978, 1984, 2011 by Biblica,
Inc. All rights reserved worldwide. Used by permission. NEW
INTERNATIONAL VERSION® and NIV® are registered trademarks
of Biblica, Inc. Use of either trademark for the offering of goods or
services requires the prior written consent of Biblica US, Inc.

Archway Publishing books may be ordered
through booksellers or by contacting:

Archway Publishing
1663 Liberty Drive
Bloomington, IN 47403
www.archwaypublishing.com
1 (888) 242-5904

Because of the dynamic nature of the Internet, any web addresses or
links contained in this book may have changed since publication and
may no longer be valid. The views expressed in this work are solely
those of the author and do not necessarily reflect the views of the
publisher, and the publisher hereby disclaims any responsibility for them.

Any people depicted in stock imagery provided by Thinkstock are
models, and such images are being used for illustrative purposes only.
Certain stock imagery © Thinkstock.

ISBN: 978-1-4808-3091-2 (sc)
ISBN: 978-1-4808-3092-9 (e)

Library of Congress Control Number: 2016907909

Print information available on the last page.

Archway Publishing rev. date: 6/1/2016

For my descendants and yours

The ones I want to leave a beautiful world to!

(Courtesy of various family members)

Contents

Foreword

"The most fortunate are those who have a wonderful capacity to appreciate again and again, freshly and naively, the basic goods of life, with awe, pleasure, wonder and even ecstasy."

—Abraham Maslow

Keeping the earth beautiful and conserving our resources has always been near and dear to my heart, and I hope it is to yours too. Over the years, I have learned a few ways we can ease our impact, or "footprint," on the earth. I hope this book will give you some ideas on how you can help, too.

I want to share a philosophy I once heard that I think is an awesome way to view the universe:

The universe was created for each and every one of us, so if there were only one person on earth, it would be the same! The earth was created *just for you*! Imagine: it could have been black and white, and it could have only one species of bird, tree, plant, flower, grass, animal, or fish. It could have had just one type of rock, have been all flat, all mountainous, all fresh water, and so on—but it would still be breathtaking! But God, or your higher power, gave so abundantly and with so much love that we should be in awe of all our wondrous gifts! The least we can do is care for it lovingly and teach our children to care for our beautiful world too.

Thank you for reading and implementing some or all of these suggestions. We all need to encourage and appreciate the efforts of each other. If you know someone who doesn't seem to know what to do, give them a copy of my book!

The efforts of one individual don't seem like much, but when you multiply it by a million, it can make a huge difference—so please know that what you do counts!

Before You Begin

Three Things You Can Do Today:

Turn off lights and water
Recycle
Use tubeless toilet paper

To help you decide where to begin, I have used the following to indicate the level of effort for each idea listed in all chapters:

Italicized items are easy to moderate, requiring a little effort or getting used to.

Italicized/bold items require a lot more effort, but they are well worth doing, if you can.

Just choose two or three items per month. Don't try too many at once or you'll get frustrated! Once you make a habit of the initial items, just add a couple more. Before you know it, you'll be saving gallons of water, millions of kilowatts, and tons of garbage!

There is a blank sheet at the end of the book where you can jot down the things you want to do and check them off as you go. You'll be amazed at how many easily become a habit and how much you will contribute to preserving our beautiful earth and her resources.

Happy implementing!

Stephens State Park, New Jersey

Treat the Earth well. We do not inherit it from our ancestors; we borrow it from our children.

—Native American saying

Chapter 1: Kitchen

(For every minute you let the water run, you waste eight quarts of water!)

Stop Buying Bottled Water: Please invest in a good water filter on your refrigerator or a bottled water service that brings reusable five gallon jugs of water to your home. If you cannot afford a water filter or service, try a Britta pitcher.

In my opinion, this is one of the worst American excesses and the epitome of arrogance and laziness. After centuries of life without bottled water, why do we now feel that we have to have bottled water? Did you know, as per a televised PSA sponsored by ecologists, that Americans throw away enough plastic water bottles in one year to go around the Earth four times?

If you don't want to do any of the above, at least you can recycle your bottles. Keep in mind, though, that recycling is not as energy efficient as just not buying them in the first place.

Cut Plastic Rings: This is something few of us think of, but most community garbage is dumped into our beautiful oceans. Fish and other creatures get caught in these rings and die, or at the least their defenses are lowered. So, please cut all the rings and openings in plastic holders before recycling them. Don't throw them in the trash.

Don't Waste Cold Water: While waiting for cold water to get hot, use it to fill a pet's water dish, water plants, rinse coffee grinds from the basket, and so on.

Don't Waste Water: Don't run the water trying to get it cold. Simply keep a pitcher of water in your refrigerator, or if you have a filter on your refrigerator, then use that. It's already cold and filtered!

Don't Overfill Your Pet's Water Dish: If you find that you constantly throw out leftover water in your pet's dish, consider putting less water in it to start with. Simply cut back a little at a time until you know what is required. If the dish is empty too often, go ahead and add a little more. Of course, the seasons will make a difference, so adjust as necessary.

Invest in a Toaster Oven: If there are only one or two people in the household, a good toaster oven can save lots of time, money, and energy. Why heat up a huge oven to broil one or two chops, heat a pizza, or bake snacks? Besides, toaster ovens cook twice as fast, are much easier to clean, and they don't heat up the whole house.

Use Your Own Bags for Groceries: Buy a few cloth bags to bring to the grocery store with you instead of using their plastic or paper bags. They are quite inexpensive, hold a lot more items, and they let you handle more weight since you carry them on your shoulder, not in your hand. They can also be used hundreds of times. Be sure to leave them in your trunk, so you always have them with you. If you must use the store's bags, please recycle them at your store—often.

Don't Put Things with Handles or Carriers in a Bag: That's why they have handles and carriers! For example: milk jugs, soft drinks, laundry soap, and dishwasher soap can all be carried separately. This even goes for large items, such as toilet paper, bags of dog food, or soda/soft drinks. It may take an extra trip or two, but it's worth saving more bags.

Quit Using Chemicals: We are all trying to remove chemicals from our bodies, so why in the world would you use harsh chemicals (bleach, ammonia, and so on) on your counters and tables? A little hot soapy water will clean them just fine! This will save some plastic bottles and lower your expenses as well. Remember, what gets on your fingers finds its way to your mouth, so use chemicals sparingly!

Disinfectants are a necessity in the operating room and in hospitals, but they're a classic example of a good thing gone bad. Nowadays many people go on cleaning frenzies in their own homes, using disinfectants everywhere. There is no need to use a disinfectant every time you wash your hands, body, or something in your environment. Overuse actually makes certain bacteria stronger and resistant to treatment (according to osteopathic physician, Dr. Mercola, at mercola.com).

Children raised in an environment of disinfectant soap and cleansers are given antibiotics that kill off all of the good and bad bacteria in their gut. They are kept away from the natural dirt, germs, viruses, and other grime of childhood and are not able to build up resistance to disease. They therefore can become vulnerable to illnesses later in life (also from Mercola.com).

Disinfectants can trigger asthma, allergies, and other health concerns. Some exposure to living bacteria is healthy and can even strengthen our immune systems (according to Envirobiolog at ewg.org).

Turn Off Electric Elements and Oven: Pans on top of the stove can be turned off three to five minutes *prior* to the food being fully cooked, since the burner will stay hot at least that long. Also, the oven can be turned off fifteen to thirty minutes *prior* to completion of baking or broiling. Each stove is different, so experiment and see how long you can quit using gas or electricity on your stove or in your oven. In case you didn't know, most electricity is generated by coal, oil or nuclear power, none of which is good for our environment.

Remember, No FOG: Do not pour fat, oil, or grease down your drain, as this clogs household and city sewer lines and is very costly to repair. Instead, pour warm FOG into an empty can or jar, wait for it to harden, and then dispose of it in your garbage. I use a coffee can or jar with a lid and keep it under my sink until it is full, and then I dispose of it.

Quit Using Multiple Bowls: Stop mixing, serving, and storing things in different bowls. Simply get some nicer-looking storage bowls and use them to mix, serve, and store items such as salad, tuna salad, chicken salad, vegetables, macaroni salad, mashed potatoes, and so forth.

Limit Use of Plastic Wrap and Aluminum Foil: Use just enough to cover the top of the container. If not soiled, use it again, especially the foil. It can be "reversed" and used again; you can tear it quite easily, too, to fit over smaller items.

Use and Rinse One Cup Per Day: Assign each member of the household one cup or glass. You can use ones with initials, different colors, shapes, or sizes, so everyone can tell them apart. Simply rinse between uses and use again and again.

Dishwasher/Dishwashing

Don't Use the Dishwasher for Pots, Pans, or Silverware: Avoid washing pots and pans in the dishwasher; that way you can use the light or normal wash cycle instead of the longer pots-and-pans cycle. If you have a smaller family and cannot fill the dishwasher in a day or two, consider washing silverware by hand. If you're like me, you hate putting away all that silverware anyway! This way you only have to deal with a few pieces at a time, and you'll never run out of clean silverware. Of course, for late-night snacks, feel free to put the one or two pieces of silverware you may use in the dishwasher. There's no sense in running it with an empty tray, either.

Use a Scrub Pad: Use a scrub pad—not just hot water—to remove stuck-on particles or grease. You can also let them soak a few minutes prior to washing.

Use a Pot, Basin, or Larger Bowl to wash the few big items and silverware you use each day. Fill it with hot, soapy water and hand-wash the larger items. This keeps the dishwasher from filling up so quickly and leaves room to rinse the dishes off in one sink. And it gives you hot, soapy water to clean up the counters, table, stovetop, high chair, spills in the refrigerator, canisters, microwave, and so on. Be sure to wipe these down prior to washing the greasy, gunky items. Wash a sink full of pots and bowls; then rinse them all quickly and put them in the drainer or second sink to drain and dry.

Don't Want a Dish Drainer on the Counter? Use an absorbent dish mat (they fold up and store easily under the sink). Or you can make it family time and have the children help by either washing or drying the dishes while you do the other. Another child could sweep the floor at the same time! The goals are togetherness and quicker cleanup, and your kitchen will look neat and clean in just a few minutes. Your children will learn some responsibility, too.

Run Dishwasher Only When It Is Full: If you find you run out of certain items sooner than others, try adding them to your hand washing items.

Never "Heat Dry": When the wash and rinse cycles are done, simply open the door, shake off the excess water on the top rack, and let the dishes dry naturally. Believe it or not, the dishes come out nicer, and you won't have any of that squeaky unnatural feel on your glassware.

Stop Using Paper Towels: Use old towels and dishcloths for cleaning. You may find you need only a roll or two of paper towels per year for especially dirty, greasy jobs. I use my old dishtowels and washcloths for inside cleanup, and when they get really bad, I move them to the garage for outside cleanup. Towels last for years and can be used over and over and over again. *Save a tree!* If you don't want to launder kitchen towels, try using EcoTowels; they are ecologically "friendly" and no trees are used to make them.

Stop Using Paper Napkins: Learn to eat properly, and teach your children, too. If you eat properly, you will have little to no food on your face or fingers. Of course, pizza, spaghetti, and barbecued ribs or chicken may be an exception. If you must have a napkin, try using linen or cloth ones; again, they can be used over and over and over and can later be recycled as rags. I also keep and use the few napkins I need by saving the ones that come with take-out food. *Save a tree!*

In case you didn't know, all paper products, including paper towels, napkins and boxes are made from trees.

Chimney Rock, North Carolina

The most important environmental issue is one that is rarely mentioned, and that is the lack of a conservation ethic in our culture.

—Gaylord Nelson

Chapter 2: Bath

(Remember, for every minute you let the water run, you waste eight quarts of water!)

Use Tubeless Toilet Paper: If you aren't doing this yet, start today! There is no reason to throw away or even recycle toilet paper tubes. This is one of the biggest wastes I can think of (except, of course, using paper towels and bottled water). Scott makes a soft two-ply toilet paper, so please use it. The cost difference is minimal!

Did you know that in America alone, we throw away enough toilet paper tubes in a year to fill the Empire State Building twice? An ad by Scott Tissue brought this to my attention. This is disgusting, wasteful, and unnecessary! I cannot think of one valid objection to changing over to tubeless toilet paper. Just think of all the resources we could save by doing this one thing, since making the tubes uses our trees and electricity, overloads our recycling processes, pollutes the environment with glue, and on and on and on.

Turn the Water Off: Wet your toothbrush, turn off the faucet, and then turn it back on when you need to rinse.

Place Some Water in the Basin: Instead of letting the water run, simply put an inch or two in the basin and use it to wet your brush to dampen your hair, to rinse off your razor while shaving, or to clean the bathroom.

Use a Towel Multiple Times: You can use a towel at least three times before you launder it. Just be sure to let it air dry between uses. Don't ball it up on the floor; it will stink. Hang it on your towel rack and let it air dry each day. The same goes for swimming pool towels.

Blow Drying/Curling Hair: Try something new! Instead of blow drying and hot curling your hair, try Velcro curlers! They have many advantages, including: 1) they last forever, 2) you don't use electricity, 3) they are better for your hair, and 4) they are easy to use: wait until your hair is just damp after washing it, roll up your hair, wait about twenty minutes, remove the curlers, and go! *Or* you can wash your hair at night and curl it in the morning. Just plug up the sink, put in an inch or so of water, wet brush/comb, dampen your hair, roll it up, wait a few minutes (I usually apply my make-up while it's drying), brush out, and *go*!

If It's Yellow, Let It Mellow: Of course you wouldn't want to do this if company is coming, but it's a good idea for every day. You can use the toilet at least twice before too much paper accumulates. So please flush less!

You Don't Need a Liner in Your Waste Basket: The bathroom garbage will not usually get wet or hold anything you can't simply wipe or rinse out. Keep plastic use to a minimum!

Recycle: Recycle toilet paper tubes (if you must use them), tampons, napkins, Kleenex, soap and toothpaste boxes, the plastic bags or containers from floss, ear swabs, and any other packaging.

You may not like these, but:

A Shower Shouldn't Take More Than Five Minutes: A shower is not meant for relaxation; it is a means to clean your body, so simply get in, get wet, lather up, rinse, and get out! Shave your legs in the sink prior to entering the shower. Simply put an inch or two of water in the basin and use it to rinse off your razor while shaving. This one simple change could save a gallon or more of precious water.

You Don't Need a Shower or Need to Wash Your Hair Every Day: Unless you sweat or actually get dirty, a daily shower is unnecessary, and it's actually unhealthy for you! It takes three days for your body oils to replenish themselves. Of course, if your work is especially dirty, a five-minute shower each day is really nice. Unless you have very oily hair, you only need to wash it once or twice a week. Water is a *precious* commodity, so please use it sparingly and wisely.

Schedule Bath Times in the Same Timeframe: By showering, one person after the other, you cut down on water waste, because the water is already warm. There is no need to wait for hot water by wasting cold water!

Younger Children Can Bathe Together! So can Mommy and Daddy, remember?

Charleston, South Carolina

When we show our respect for other living things, they respond with respect for us.

—Arapaho Proverb

Chapter 3: Laundry

Wash Only Full Loads: If you must wash one item, ask yourself, can I hand wash it? If you must wash a few items, be sure to use the smallest load option on your machine.

Use Cold Water & Biodegradable Detergent: They make wonderful cold water and biodegradable detergents now. Don't waste energy heating up the water or pollute the water any more than you have to.

Clean Filters Often: This not only helps with the washer and dryer efficiency, but dryer lint buildup is a major cause of home fires! Be sure to clean the entire vent from the dryer to the outside of the house, at least once a year!

Try Using Less Than a Complete Drying Cycle: I discovered this by accident! Then I tried it on purpose and, believe it or not, I found that if you set your drying cycle on just a bit more than half the usual time, your clothes will actually be dry, especially if you don't overload the dryer.

Try Using a Clothesline*: Again, this is a big one. But do you remember that wonderful smell of clothes dried outside? Better than a dryer sheet! Even if you only hang out your sheets and towels, what a savings that would be! They even make clotheslines that retract, so you don't have to put up with the old ugly lines in your yard.

Catalina Island, California

What you do affects our environment.
Start conserving today.

Mary Stanowicz-Freeman

Chapter 4: General Household

Adjust Your Thermostat: If you find yourself chilly in the summer, raise your thermostat a couple of degrees. I can't believe how many people I see using blankets in the summer! The same goes for winter; if you find yourself too warm, lower it. It's amazing the natural resources and money you can save by living comfortably, yet not *wastefully.*

Adjust Your Hot Water Temperature: Here again, if you are burning yourself when your water gets hot, lower the thermostat on your hot water heater.

Turn Off Lights Every Time You Leave a Room: Turn off the lights, since you may get sidetracked after you leave a room and not return for quite awhile.

Order Your Newspaper Online: Stop getting a printed newspaper and instead subscribe to an online version. Obviously, this saves trees, ink, gas for distribution, recycling or landfill costs, litter, etc. Besides, if there is a particular item you want a hard copy of (usually of a family story), you can print that one article for yourself. And you can use Groupon for any coupons you may want; I believe there are apps, too.

Keep Shades Drawn: Keep your shades/blinds/curtains closed or just slightly open, with the slats turned upward in summer to keep the heat out and downward in winter to allow the sun in. During extreme heat and cold, this will save you a lot of money and will help conserve our energy supply. In more pleasant weather, please feel free to turn off the heating, ventilating, and air conditioning (HVAC) and open them and your windows wide!

Seal Doors and Windows: Be sure your windows and doors have weather stripping and/or caulking. This prevents the outside air from getting into your home, keeps you more comfortable, and helps keep your HVAC costs down.

Change HVAC Filters: Make a habit of changing them on the same day each month; that way you won't forget, and your heat and air conditioning will run more efficiently and economically.

Leave Your Ceiling Fans On: Believe it or not, this helps with heating and cooling costs in the rooms you use frequently. For rooms you seldom use, this does not apply; simply close the vent and the door. There is a little switch on the light portion of your fan or on the fan unit itself if you do not have lights. This switch changes the airflow from down to up for the proper circulation of air. Put the switch in the down position for summer and in the up position for winter. I remember this easily: D comes before U, and S comes before W in the alphabet—*down and summer* versus *up and winter.*

By using ceiling fans in the summer, your home will feel up to eight degrees cooler and save up to 40 percent on air conditioning costs. In winter, they make you feel warmer and can save you up to 15 percent on heating costs (according to delmarfans.com).

Repair Leaky Faucets, Toilets, and Hoses: Do this as soon as possible. A new washer will usually do the trick.

Limit Your Garbage Bag Use: If you cannot eliminate the use of garbage bags altogether (by just using the can and rinsing it out), please at least *fill them up*! Compact them frequently so you can fit more in one bag. As a challenge, try to cut your use by half. What an accomplishment that would be!

Save and Reuse Boxes: Save boxes, especially Christmas and/or gift boxes. Use one of your larger shipping boxes, and use it each year to store the boxes for use throughout the year.

Shop a Day or Two before Your Scheduled Garbage Pick-Up: This way, you can dispose of items in your refrigerator or cabinets before they become offensive. Before you put your groceries away, clean out the outdated items, and don't forget to recycle or compost anything you can.

Disposable or Not: Before you buy disposable items, like the ones listed throughout this book (napkins, razors, water bottles, etc.), please think twice and ask yourself, *couldn't I use a reusable one?* They are usually much nicer, and they last for years!

Stop Using Freezer Bags: Buy some inexpensive Glad containers to freeze your meat portions and/or leftovers. They will last a long, long time—especially if you hand wash them.

Use Cloth Diapers: I know this is a tough one! It takes a serious heart and a bit more effort than most of the others. I realize they may not always be an option (most day care centers don't allow them), or may be a real inconvenience (like when travelling)—but would you consider using them while you are at home? They really are not that difficult to deal with, and they will save you hundreds of dollars per child and thousands of trees, even if you only use them while you're at home!

Grand Canyon, Arizona

We're reaching the point where the Earth
will have to end the burden we've placed on
her, if we don't lift the burden ourselves.

—Steven M. Greer

Chapter 5: Vehicle

Do Not Idle Your Car: The only exception here may be if you live in a very cold climate and you need to warm up your engine for a minute or two (not ten). You'll live! The engine heats up and the A/C cools down in a couple minutes, and this will cut your contribution to pollution and fuel waste.

Plan Your Errands: Before you leave your home, pause a moment and *plan the route* you should take to accomplish your errands without zigzagging around town.

Walk or Ride a Bike: If your destination is within a mile or so, consider riding your bike or walking! Save energy and money and also get some valuable exercise! Remember, though: safety first.

Grocery Shop Once a Week: Or less. With a little planning, you shouldn't have to run to the store every day. Keep a list handy and jot things down as you run out of them, or that you don't buy every week. Be sure to add the items you may need for a new recipe, too.

Dispose of Oil Properly: Take your used oil (in a clean container with a lid) and oil filters to a nearby recycling center. Some auto parts stores and gas stations will accept it and recycle it for you. Do not discard it on your lawn or in the trash, as these are major toxic pollutants and need to be treated accordingly.

Don't Litter: This is totally unnecessary! Keep a waste container in your car, and simply empty it when you get home or to your destination

Smokers: Please invest in an ashtray, and empty it often. No one wants to look at your butts littering the highway. If your ashtray is full, simply roll down the window, roll off the hot end and excess tobacco, and place the butt in the ashtray. Be responsible and make sure it's safe.

Use a Car Wash: This one is good news! It's actually cheaper, easier, and more ecologically responsible to use a good car wash! Be sure they recycle their water and use biodegradable soap. Think of the time, water and energy you will save!

Home car washing releases contaminated water directly into the environment or into storm drains intended for rainwater. This pollutes our rivers, lakes, streams, and harbors, and also wastes valuable water. A basic car wash is very reasonable, but be sure they use recycled water and biodegradable detergents.

Carpool: I don't know why, but most people do not like to carpool. It has to be one of the most efficient ways to help the environment! If you need your car one day, you can simply let your "copilot" know the night before. Won't you try it at least two or three days per week? Ask your human resources department for assistance; they can organize it for the employees and get people excited about saving energy and lowering pollution. At least I know my niece Katie would!

Carpool, Small Company: If your company is too small, consider asking your human resources department or supervisor to check with local area small businesses to see whether they would be interested in forming a program or add your company's employees to their program. Remember—where there's a will, there's a way.

Natural Bridge, Virginia

Trees are poems that the earth writes upon the sky.

—Kahlil Gibran, *Sand and Foam*

Chapter 6: Outside

Use Native Plants: Native plants are acclimated to the area in which you live, so they require less additional resources to flourish (less fertilizer, water, soil changes, etc.). They go from seed to sprout to flower and back to seed again—naturally!

If You Have a Dog: You can use one doggie bag for more than one "poop." Dogs usually take at least two per walk. Simply twist the top of the bag and use it again before knotting it. If they go in your yard, invest in a good pooper-scooper, and use one bag for all the waste.

Swimming Pool Towels: You can use a towel at least three times before you launder it. Just be sure to let it hang dry between uses; don't ball it up on the deck—it will stink. Hang it on your railing or chair and let it air dry each day. The same goes for bath towels.

Don't Litter: This is totally unnecessary! Just carry it or put it in your pocket or purse and simply empty it when you come across a waste container. They are everywhere.

Chewing Gum: If you have to, swallow it! Or dispose of it properly before spitting it out becomes a necessity. You could carry a tissue with you and use that, and then discard it when disposals are available.

Camping & Beaches: I can't think of any more important places to clean up litter than when you go camping or to the beach. Be sure to clean up after yourselves and any messes left by less considerate people. I know you cannot clean up the entire area, but could you do a ten, or twenty-five-square-foot area? We always did, and you can too!

Cigarettes: Carry an empty cigarette pack with you; simply roll off the hot end and excess tobacco, and then place the butt in the box. If you do not have a box or anything to put it into, put it in your pocket! Dispose of them when you find an ashtray or waste receptacle. Please keep our streets clean. Be responsible and make sure it is safe first. Don't forget to crush the hot end so you don't start a fire!

Plant a Tree: Plant a native, hardwood tree in your yard. It's a great way to give back to Mother Nature. What better gift can we give? They're beautiful, and they give us shade and oxygen. If you can't fit one in your budget, ask for one as a gift for Mother's Day, Father's Day, your birthday, anniversary, or other special occasion. Your children will love to watch them grow! I remember the one my brother planted when I was six years old. Over fifty years later, I still love to go home and see how big it has gotten. I feel like it's now part of me! My children love to see the ones we've planted as well. Somehow it makes you feel like you have actually accomplished something, and you have!

Use a Rain Barrel: Place a container under one of your downspouts and collect rainwater from the roof to use in your garden! This will not only save on water but also it's fun to see how much you can collect.

Newport Beach, California

Water and air, the two essential fluids on which all life depends, have become global garbage cans..

—Jacques-Yves Cousteau

Chapter 7: Recycling

Understand Recycling Symbols: A good place to find this information is at www.goodhousekeeping.com.

Check with Your Local Waste Company: Check to see what they will accept in their recycling program. If there are items you would like to recycle that they do not currently accept, *ask* them to consider accepting them in the future. Communities upgrade their recycling programs often and take into consideration requests from their residents.

Crush Boxes and Cans: The more you compact your items, the more you can fit into the provided containers.

Rinse Cans and Bottles: They don't have to be sanitized, but please remove the chunks! No one wants to deal with gross waste.

Don't Forget to Recycle!

Again, Plastic Bottles: If you must buy bottled water and/or soft drinks, etc., *please recycle* them! We don't need to go around the earth three times with this waste (which is what America does) when all it takes is simply choosing the correct container to place them in! This goes for cans and glass as well, of course.

Mail inserts and envelopes

Junk Mail

Glass and metal (tin or aluminum) cans

All boxes: Remove and dispose of the bags and pouches that contained the actual food product in your garbage container, and recycle the outside boxes from cereal, packaged potatoes, rice dishes, crackers, frozen dinner boxes, and so on.

You can also recycle pasta boxes, dog treat boxes, outer wrappings on wrappings (bag around microwave popcorn, cellophane wrappings around boxes for things like tea bags) and many other items. Before you discard anything, *think* about whether recycling is an option.

Magazines

Newspapers

Cardboard boxes, including shipping, shoe boxes, etc.

Consign your used items: Clothes, shoes, purses, suits, coats, and other items can be consigned. Many of the items we discard are still good, and someone would be thrilled to have them, especially our dress clothes. You will be making desired items available to the less fortunate, keeping someone in business, and you will make more money than you would at a garage sale.

Give to Charity: If you don't want to go to a consignment store, consider giving your items to a battered women's shelter (contact your local sheriff), Goodwill, Salvation Army, or a homeless shelter.

Scott's Garden

What you take from the earth, you must
give back. That's nature's way.

—Chris d'Lacey, *The Fire Within*

Chapter 8: Composting

Love gardening? Have lots of plants? Have a yard?

Choose a Compost Bin: You can choose from any number of bins, some of which come with a tumbling device, so you don't have to turn it yourself. You can also make your own out of a plastic container, drilling a number of holes on all sides, or you can simply put it in your yard.

Select a location for your bin: Pick a place that is downwind of your home (compost piles can smell), one that is easily accessible, level and well-drained, not on concrete or paving. Be sure to remove any grass or plants; these will be your first items to compost. Rototill the area to about six to eight inches, and you're ready to go.

Start with: A layer of brush, twigs, hay or straw, and then begin adding your brown and green waste.

Brown waste: Items such as leaves, woody prunings, egg shells, paper, cardboard, coffee grounds, and tea bags.

Green waste: Items such as vegetable and fruit peelings and scraps, grass clippings, as well as hedge and green plant cuttings. Avoid weeds, as we really don't want to spread these around our garden.

Turn your pile: Every two weeks or so, turn your pile. The more you mix it up, the faster you'll have finished compost.

Do not add: Meat, bones, poultry, fish, fat, whole eggs, dairy products, treated wood, or feces of any kind—pet or human. (Sorry I had to mention this, but you would be amazed!)

When it's ready: It takes anywhere from one to twelve months to produce finished compost. It is ready when it is dark, crumbly, and has a pleasant, earthy smell. Check other authors and/or the Internet for more information on this, as I am not an expert! What I know, I learned from my sister-in-law, Joyce Seber Stanowicz.

Can be used for: House plants, fertilizer, flower and vegetable beds, and around trees—just to mention a few.

Happy composting! Your plants and the earth will thank you.

Lake Tahoe, California

No water—no trees

no trees—no air

no air—no life.

—Mary Stanowicz-Freeman

Chapter 9: Public

Ask at Your Grocery Store: Ask the manager at your local grocery store to put a large banner on their front window that states *Don't Forget Your Bags!* in big, bright, bold letters! You would be amazed how many trips back to the car this has saved me! Of course, you do have to buy a few first. Just think of the thousands of plastic bags we can save by doing this one simple thing!

Ask Your City Government: Ask your city government to improve their recycling programs by accepting more items in your bin or at the curb.

No Recycling Program: Work with your homeowner association (HOA) or city to create one! A good source of information or assistance would be through one of your local recycling centers. Ask them to make a presentation to your HOA/City on the costs, uses, and benefits of a recycling program. You may have to make the arrangements, but it is imperative that we all recycle as much as possible, and it would be a very rewarding experience for you as well!

This will work at apartment and swimming complexes as well.

Acknowledgments

I would like to take a moment to thank my mom and dad, especially my mother for passing on her love of nature. Also, to my wonderful family and friends—for all their love and support throughout my life, particularly my precious daughter who encouraged me, believed in my dream, and contributed in many ways, including financially, to the publication of this book. I could not have done it without her. My family knows who they are (and I include my in-laws and extended family!), but I would like to mention my friends by name: Star Pietrowskowicz-March, Louella Gilbertson, and Glori Gillespie! Thank you for all the encouraging words and love!

This work would never have come to fruition without the strength and perseverance the Holy Spirit gave me. I thank the Lord for helping me with my dream, and hopefully this is His plan for me.

Remember, God's very first command was to take care of the earth (Genesis 1:28–31). If it was that important to him, it should be important to us! Also, in Psalms 115:16 it states: "The highest heavens belong to the Lord, but the earth He has given to mankind." If it belongs to us, we need to care for it every way we can.

Let's all do our part!

God bless each and every one of you who tries to implement some or all of these suggestions. I know it may take time, so just pick two or three to start each month, and before you know it you will be making a huge difference and a great contribution for your descendants and all mankind!

Remember, as we are one with nature and we are part of each other, it is our obligation to care for the Earth at least as well as we care for ourselves.

What's the use of a fine house if you haven't got a tolerable planet to put it on?

—Henry David Thoreau, *Familiar Letters*

Why not track the items you want to incorporate, and add your own too. I'm sure I missed some!

Final Thought

Buck Hill, New Jersey

It is not so much for its beauty that the forest makes a claim upon men's hearts, as for that subtle something— that quality of air, that emanation from old trees, that so wonderfully changes and renews a weary spirit.

—Robert Louis Stevenson

References

All quotes came from the internet, except my own. I simply googled environmental quotes

Plastics: ecowatch.com and ecologycenter.org

Disinfectants: mercola.com and envirobiolog@ewg.com

Ceiling fans: delmarfans.com

Compost: compost-info-guide.com, planetnatural.com or realsimple.com

Recycling Symbols found at www.goodhousekeeping.com

Google any topic and search innumerable websites.

Additional Resources

Compost information also from my sister-in-law, Joyce Seber-Stanowicz

All photographs (except those in chapter 9) are by Sientje Freeman. Cover photo is of author's back yard in Charlotte, NC

Chapter 9 photograph is by Scott Stanowicz.

Information on toilet paper rolls filling Empire State Building is from an ad by Scott Tissue.